Chess

A musical

(London stage version)

Music by Benny Andersson and Björn Ulvaeus

Lyrics by Tim Rice

Based on an idea by Tim Rice

Samuel French — London
New York - Toronto - Hollywood

ISBN 0 573 08095 X

CHESS

First performed at the Prince Edward Theatre, London, on 14th May, 1986 with the following cast:

Frederick Trumper	Murray Head
Florence Vassy	Elaine Paige
Anatoly Sergievsky	Tommy Korberg
Walter de Courcey	Kevin Colson
Alexander Molokov	John Turner
Arbiter	Tom Jobe
Svetlana Sergievskaya	Siobhan McCarthy

The Company: Leo Andrew, Julie Armstrong, Yvonne Bachem, Julia Birch, Richard Courtice, Catherine Coffee, Annie Cox, Hugh Craig, Geoffrey Dallamore, Carol Duffy, Garrick Forbes, Wayne Fowkes, Aliki Georgiou, Philip Griffith, Peter Karrie, Donna King, Madeline Loftin, Patrick Long, Kim Lonsdale, Richard Lyndon, Richard Mitchell, Gail Mortley, Kerri Murphy, Mhairi Nelson, Anita Pashley, William Pool, Jane Powell, Grainne Rennihan, Richard Sampson, Jacqui Scott, Duncan Smith, Sandy Strallen, Suzanne Thomas, Sally Ann Triplett, Oke Wambu, Hilary Western, Paul Wilson

Directed by Trevor Nunn
Designed by Robin Wagner

SYNOPSIS OF SCENES AND MUSICAL NUMBERS

PROLOGUE

1 **The Story of Chess**

ACT I

SCENE 1 A station in Merano, Italy

2 **Merano**

SCENE 2 Frederick and Florence's suite/Conference room

3 **Commie Newspapers**

4 **Press Conference**

SCENE 3 Molokov's suite

5 **Anatoly & Molokov**

6 **Where I Want to Be**

SCENE 4 The Arbiter's chambers

7 **Diplomats**

8 **The Arbiter**

9 **Hymn**

10 **The Merchandisers**

SCENE 5 The arena

Chess (instrumental)

11 **The Arbiter (reprise)**

12 **A Model of Decorum and Tranquillity (Quartet)**

13 **Florence & Molokov**

SCENE 6 A television studio and control room

14 **1956 — Budapest Is Rising**

15 **Nobody's Side**

SCENE 7 The Merano Mountain Inn

16 ***Der Kleine Franz***

17 **Mountain Duet**

SCENE 8 The arena

Chess (2nd version: instrumental)

SCENE 9 Frederick and Florence's suite/The Arbiter's chambers
18 Florence Quits
19 Pity the Child

SCENE 10 A consulate in Merano
20 Embassy Lament
21 Heaven Help My Heart

SCENE 11 A station in Merano, Italy
22 Anatoly and the Press
23 Anthem

ACT II

SCENE 1 The streets of Bangkok, Thailand
24 Golden Bangkok (ballet/instrumental)
25 One Night in Bangkok

SCENE 2 Anatoly and Florence's suite
26 One More Opponent
27 You and I

SCENE 3 Molokov's suite
28 The Soviet Machine

SCENE 4 A television studio
29 Interview

SCENE 5 The foyer of the Oriental Hotel, Bangkok
30 The Deal
31 I Know Him So Well

SCENE 6 A Buddhist temple
32 Talking Chess

SCENE 7 The arena
33 Endgame

SCENE 8 The arena/airport
34 You and I (reprise)
35 Walter & Florence

EPILOGUE
36 Epilogue

The music for *Chess* is available on hire from Samuel French Ltd.

CHARACTERS

Frederick Trumper, American Grandmaster
Florence Vassy, Frederick's lover/second
Anatoly Sergievsky, Russian Grandmaster
Walter de Courcey, head of the American delegation
Alexander Molokov, head of the Russian delegation
Arbiter
Svetlana Sergievskaya

Citizens of Merano, Reporters, Delegates, Civil Servants and various other roles to be played by The Company

The action takes place in and around the arenas of the World Chess Championships in Merano, Italy, and one year later in Bangkok, Thailand

Time — the Cold War Era of the early 1980s

There have been so many alterations to the structure of *Chess* during its turbulent history that we are reluctant to present any variation of the work to the public as the definitive one. The version of the show within these pages is, however, a close approximation to the form of the successful London production of 1986.

Anyone mounting a production of *Chess* should not be afraid of making cuts or of changing the order of some of the songs and scenes. In particular, reference to the original recording of the work (RCA CHESS PD 70500) may inspire some alternate approaches to the version presented in this book. Some scenes such as Act I, Scene 2 and "*Der Kleine Franz*" can be cut entirely without weakening the whole.

I have always felt that, musically at least, the positioning of "The Story of Chess", used as a prologue in the London stage production, is most effective as the centre piece of "You and I", as per the original recording. The lyrics of this alternative are included herein. "Pity the Child" and "Heaven Help My Heart" are two other prominent songs which have left their album berths to no great discernible profit.

The greatest benefit of the short-lived Broadway production of 1988 was the creation of one brand new song, entitled "Someone Else's Story". This can be heard on the Broadway cast recording, with sheet music available from Samuel French Ltd. The lyrics are in this volume as an optional extra. Where to place this song for Florence within the context of the London version is tricky. Provided it is not felt that the first half is becoming overloaded with ballads, it fits well plot-wise immediately before or immediately after Scene 8 in Act I. Or it could conceivably replace "Nobody's Side", which in turn could move to the very end of the show, replacing the short Epilogue — an experiment that worked well when *Chess* toured the UK after its West End run. Of course, I must point out that it is impossible to grant permission for any further songs or scenes not included in this book to be added.

Whatever sequence of songs and scenes you choose, we wish you well and thank you for your interest. When in real doubt, refer back to the original album — first thoughts are often best and in many respects I wish we had never changed a note of it!

Tim Rice
November 1993

ACT I
Prologue

Song 1: "The Story of Chess"

Arbiter and Chorus

Each game of chess means there's one less
Variation left to be played
Each day got through means one or two
Less mistakes remain to be made

Each game of chess means there's one less
Variation left to be played
Each day got through means one or two
Less mistakes remain to be made

Not much is known
Of early days of chess beyond a fairly vague report
That fifteen hundred years ago two princes fought
Though brothers, for a Hindu throne

Their mother cried
For no-one really likes their offspring fighting to the death
She begged them stop the slaughter with her every breath
But sure enough one brother died

Sad beyond belief
She told her winning son
You have caused such grief
I can't forgive this evil thing you've done

He tried to explain
How things had really been
But he tried in vain
No words of his could mollify the Queen

And so he asked the wisest men he knew
The way to lessen her distress
They told him he'd be pretty certain to impress
By using model soldiers on
A chequered board to show it was his brother's fault
They thus invented chess

Chess displayed no inertia
Soon spread to Persia, then west
Next the Arabs refined it,
Thus redesigned, it progressed

Still further yet
And when Constantinople fell in fourteen fifty-three
One would have noticed every other refugee
Included in his bags a set

Once in the hands
And in the minds of
Leading figures of the Renaissance
The spirit and the speed of chess
Made swift advance through
All of Europe's vital lands

Where, we must record
The game was further changed right across the board
The western touch upon the
Pieces ranged

King and queen and rook
And bishop, knight and pawn
All took on the look
We know today, the modern game was born

And in the end
We see a game that started by mistake in Hindustan
And boosted in the main by what is now Iran
Become the simplest and most complicated
Pleasure yet devised

For just the kind of mind
Who would appreciate this well-researched
And fascinating yarn

Arbiter The International Chess Federation, of which I have the honour of being President, announces that the next World Championship will take place in Merano, Italy. The current world champion, Frederick Trumper, of the United States of America, will defend his title against Anatoly Sergievsky, of the Soviet Union. The first player to achieve six victories will be declared champion. The first game will begin on March twenty-seventh.

ACT I

Scene 1

A station in Merano, Italy

Is this The Sound of Music? *Tyrolean hats, leather pants, yodels and dancing. Snow-capped mountain peaks and icy rivers. Narrow, crowded, colourful streets of shops. Grapes and the benefits of the spa. The Mayor and Citizens are waiting for an important arrival at the station*

Song 2: "Merano"

Mayor and Citizens

Oh, light the heart
That lingers in Merano
Merano! The spa no
Connoisseur of spas would miss
So healthy
Highly recommended
Is this sweet metropolis
Mental and physical bliss!

The gods have smiled
And blessèd is Merano
Merano! There are no
Fitter burghers to be found
Such vigour!
Take the time to taste us
We'll give you a welcome that's typically Tyrol

For then we are sure of our ground
Right now we're Italian — we used to be German
The border keeps shifting around

Mayor (solo)
Speaking as one of the patriarchs
I don't mind taking your lira or marks

Mayor and Citizens
Oh, I get high when I saunter by
The mountains of Merano
Rosy-cheeked Merano
Flourishing to a fault
The sparkling streams, the bracing air
The therapeutic salt
I'd have to be carried away to call a halt!

Oh, I feel great in this bouncing state
O hail to thee, Merano
Hearty hale Merano
Any objections? Nein!
Where breathing in will turn you on
Where water tastes like wine
Get out your get up and go and get in line
It's living your life in a show by
Rodgers and Hammerstein!

Oh sad the soul
Who passes by Merano
Merano: so far no
Soul has ever passed us by
They love us
Why not stay forever?
Oh so many reasons why
All those in favour say, "Ay"
Ay!

So sing a song
Let's hear it for Merano
Merano! Soprano,
Alto, tenor, bass agree
We're wholesome

What a happy haven
This is a place where your arteries soften
Cholesterol hasn't a chance
From mountain to valley the natural goodness
Is fighting pollution's advance

Mayor (solo) So come to us and feel the force
All major credit cards taken, of course

Mayor and Citizens Oh, I get high when I saunter by
The mountains of Merano
Rosy-cheeked Merano
Flourishing to a fault
The sparkling streams, the bracing air
The therapeutic salt
I'd have to be carried away to call a halt!

Once in a while all the gods will smile
On little old Merano
Humble shy Merano
Suddenly hits the press
And I report with all the pride
And joy that I possess
Half of the world and his wife
Has our address
Our little town will be rife
With games of chess!

There is a whistling/yodelling/orchestral interlude during which a train rushes through the station

Get out your get up and go and get in line
It's living your life in a show ...

Another train rushes into the station and stops. The man more responsible than any other for the enormous interest in a World Chess Championship match, the current world champion, the American Frederick Trumper, gets off the train and pushes his way through the mêlée. He brushes aside the official reception. He is flanked by his lover/second Florence Vassy and two or three other members of his delegation (males), one of whom is also the man who is ostensibly head of the American TV production company covering the event, Walter de Courcey

Frederick surveys the town, its people and its visitors with patronizing amusement

Frederick What a scene! What a joy!
What a lovely sight
When my game is the big sensation!
Has the mob's sporting taste
Altered overnight?
Have they found new sophistication?

Not yet! They just want to see
If the nice guy beats the bum
If it's East-West
And the money's sky-high
They all come

Florence! (*He takes a photograph of Florence*)

You can raise all you want
If you raise the roof
Scream and shout and the gate increases
Break the rules — break the bank
I'm the living proof
They don't care how I move my pieces

I know I'm the best there is
But all they want is a show
Well that's all right — I'll be glad to oblige
S.R.O. ... S.R.O. ...

Frederick and his entourage leave

Determined to have their welcoming ceremony, the Mayor and Citizens give the full works to a bewildered stranger who happened to be on the same train

Mayor and Citizens

Oh, I get high when I saunter by
The mountains of Merano
Rosy-cheeked Merano
Flourishing to a fault
The sparkling streams, the bracing air
The therapeutic salt
I'd have to be carried away to call a halt!

Oh, I feel great in this bouncing state
O hail to thee, Merano
Hearty hale Merano
Any objections? Nein!
Where breathing in will turn you on
Where water tastes like wine
Get out your get up and go and get in line
It's living your life in a show by
Rodgers and Hammerstein!

Now for the sell
We put the ice into paradise
We are the salt of the earth
Sound as a bell
Check out the waters
And check out the hygiene
At which we excel
Check into an hotel
And schnell
Body and soul get well!

Scene 2

The Palace Hotel, Merano. Frederick and Florence's suite

Frederick is alone, playing chess against a computer

Computer Knight D-five.
Frederick Bishop A-five. Check.

Florence enters with a bundle of newspapers

Song 3: "Commie Newspapers"

Florence Well, we can't complain you've been ignored by the press
Frederick What'd they say? What'd they say?
Florence They're not too polite ——
Frederick They say I'm a shit?
Florence Well, yes.
They've pulled you to pieces in five different languages.

Frederick goes up to Florence, kisses her quickly, and starts looking though some papers

Here we are — *The Times*: you "thrive on unpleasantness".

Frederick finds this amusing, and Florence seems to as well

Le Monde: "Freddie Trumper — *La Honte des Echècs*."
Frederick I don't believe that they can't see my game
I'm like that tennis player — what's his name?
They love to hate me and for us that's dollars!
Florence *Die Stern*: "*Der Grössliche Skandal des Schachs*."
Frederick Hey look — here's a piece that some idiot's done on you
"Florence Vassy — petite Hungarian-born English woman,
His gentle companion" — huh! If they only knew!
Florence (*pushing him on to the bed*) What do you mean? You know I'm always gentle with you, Freddie ...
Both "She stands by her champion ——"
Frederick I like this!
Both "— whose demands are so infantile —"
Frederick I don't like this! (*He throws the paper away*)
Florence If you don't like it then it's up to you
They like the Russian — they could like you too.
Frederick Commie newspapers!
Of course the bastards all support the Russian
Florence (*teasingly*) But Sergievsky seems a sweet opponent —
So why do you abuse him all the time?
Freddie, I love you very much but just for once don't go on about the Russians at the press conference, OK?

Frederick All Soviets deserve abuse!

Florence exits

This scene dissolves into one of the hotel's conference rooms. A gaggle of reporters, photographers, interviewers and TV personnel are assembled to speak to Frederick, who is facing the gathering. Florence has not yet arrived

Song 4: "Press Conference"

Reporter 1 Does your opponent deserve such abuse?
Frederick All Soviets deserve abuse!
Reporter 2 But even you must concede he can play
Frederick He's the best red on the circuit, sure, I'll give him that ...
Reporter 1 He hasn't lost for a long time. He could be a tough nut to crack
Frederick Listen, if he gets one game off me, it's because I want to keep the press interest going ...
Reporters Why do you persist
With vicious attacks
Ungracious remarks re
Opponents? It smacks
Of a lack of conviction, admit
You're under duress
And that your only skill left
Is for money, not chess

If Soviet life's
As grim as you claim
Then how come their boys are
So good at the game?
Though you swear the American dream
Is clearly the best
You're no advertisement for
Life and times in the West

Florence enters

Reporter 4 Why did you risk the whole match breaking down?

Frederick I don't know what you're saying, what are you — what are you implying?
Reporter 1 All your outrageous demands, self-conceit ——
Frederick I don't see anything outrageous in demanding what I'm worth!
Reporter 5 They pay you all that you ask for
And then you demand even more ——
Frederick I'm the reason you're all here! Who's ever heard of Sergievsky?
Reporters It's hard to believe what we're reporting
Why so disparaging? Not very sporting
Frederick Are the Communists sporting? My God ——
Reporters Tell all this to the United Nations
Are you an asset to East-West relations?
Frederick What is this? What have the Russians ever done for East-West relations? Do you guys have any serious questions?
Reporter 6 What's your impression of our little town?
Frederick Rather cold and dull. As I expected.
Reporter 2 Where would you rather have played? Leningrad?
Frederick Leningrad was an insulting Soviet suggestion ——
Reporter 3 They only tried to be friendly
They would have played in New York
Frederick Aw, c'mon — you know as well as I do what their motives were!
Reporters You protest too much, we see your ploy, a
Big noise to hide your fears — pure paranoia
Frederick I'm not paranoid — they're out to get me!
Reporters Tell all this to the United Nations
Are you an asset to East-West relations?
Frederick Jesus ...
Reporter 7 Will you be quitting for good if you lose?

Frederick stares at the questioner, but makes no reply

Reporter 2 How come your second's a girl, lover-boy?
Frederick (*after a double-take*) What'd you say?
Reporter 2 How come your second's a girl, lover-boy?

Frederick rushes at the Reporter and hits him

Frederick storms off

Pandemonium breaks out, from which emerges:

Reporters

Well what did I say
He's out of his tree
He's finally flipped
And between you and me
He's no hope of retaining his crown
In this frame of mind
In fact he shouldn't have come here
He should have resigned

Florence desperately tries to restore order. As the Reporters reprise their final lines, she dominates their words with a powerful outburst

Florence

Smile, you got your first exclusive story
Now you can bask in his reflected glory
Naked, unprovoked Yankee aggression
Oh, what a credit to your great profession!

The scene changes during the Reporters' final words

Reporters

Much better to quit
While still number one
Than crash to defeat
Reputation undone
Though he's proved to himself
It's a Communist plot
If you ask me it's the money that did it
And started the rot
It's sad that the best
His country's produced
Is crumbling in front
Of our eyes and reduced
To a mindless abuse and assault
On all of mankind
I think he shouldn't have come back
He should have resigned

Scene 3

Molokov's suite in Merano

Anatoly Sergievsky, the Russian challenger to Frederick, and the head of his delegation, Alexander Molokov, have been watching the press conference on TV. The image of Florence's face during her final speech to the Reporters is now on the screen. Newspapers with all the stories about Frederick are lying about

Molokov The man is utterly mad — believe me, Anatoly, you're playing a lunatic.

Anatoly That's the problem. He's a brilliant lunatic and you can't tell which way he'll jump. Like his game, he's impossible to analyse — you can't dissect him, predict him. Which, of course, means he's not a lunatic at all.

Song 5: "Anatoly & Molokov"

Molokov What we've just seen's a pathetic display
From a man who's beginning to crack
He's afraid — he knows he isn't the player he was
And he won't get it back

Anatoly Nonsense!
Why do my seconds
Always want to believe
Third-rate propaganda?

Molokov My friend, please relax
We're all on your side
You know how you need us

Anatoly I don't need my army of so-called "advisers"
And "helpers" to tell me
The man who's revitalized chess single-handed
Is more or less out of his brain
When it's very clear he's sane

Molokov Listen! We don't underestimate anyone
We won't get caught in that trap
After all, winning or losing reflects on us all

Anatoly Aah, don't give me that crap!
I win — no-one else does
And *I* take the rap if I lose

Molokov It's not quite that simple
The whole world's tuned in
We're all on display
We're not merely sportsmen

Anatoly Oh please, don't start spouting that old party line
Yes I know it's your job but
Just get out and get me a chess-playing second
In thirty-six hours we begin
That is, if you want to win!

Molokov Wanting's not sufficient — we have to know, we have to make sure. All men have a weakness and his is that woman; take her and you win the game!

Anatoly So you think I can't win otherwise?

Molokov I'm not saying that — I'm just making certain. And she's attractive ... then there is her intriguing family history — Hungary, nineteen fifty-six and all that ——

Anatoly I'm a chess player, Mr Molokov — you go and play these other games!

Molokov leaves, displeased

Anatoly switches off the TV. He wanders over to a chess board and moves some pieces

Song 6: "Where I Want to Be"

Who needs a dream?
Who needs ambition?
Who'd be the fool
In my position?
Once I had dreams
Now they're obsessions
Hopes became needs
Lovers possessions

Then they move in
Oh, so discreetly
Slowly at first
Smiling too sweetly
I opened doors

They walked right through them
Called me their friend
I hardly knew them

Now I'm where I want to be and who I want to be
And doing what I always said I would
And yet I feel I haven't won at all
Running for my life and never looking back
In case there's someone right behind to
Shoot me down and say he always knew I'd fall

When the crazy wheel slows down
Where will I be? Back where I started

Don't get me wrong
I'm not complaining
Times have been good
Fast, entertaining
But what's the point?
If I'm concealing
Not only love
All other feeling

Now I'm where I want to be and who I want to be
And doing what I always said I would
And yet I feel I haven't won at all
Running for my life and never looking back
In case there's someone right behind to
Shoot me down and say he always knew I'd fall

When the crazy wheel slows down
Where will I be? Back where I started

A Russian enters

Russian Molokov tells me you want to play chess. I have one hour before the delegates' conference ——

Anatoly Go to hell!

Scene 4

The Arbiter's chambers

The Arbiter has summoned the two opposing delegations to his room immediately prior to the first game in the match. The Soviet delegation consists of about a dozen people led by Molokov. The American Delegation consists of Florence (not yet present), Walter and two genuine other seconds

Song 7: "Diplomats"

All Delegates No-one can deny that these are difficult times
No-one can deny that these are difficult times
Molokov Mr de Courcey!
Walter Mr Molokov —
Russians It's the US versus USSR
Yet we more or less are —
Americans No-one can deny that these are difficult times
Russians — to our credit putting all that aside
We have swallowed our pride
Americans These are very dangerous and difficult times
It really doesn't matter who comes out on top
Walter Who gets the chop
Americans No-one's way of life is threatened by a flop
All Delegates But we're gonna smash their bastard
Make him wanna change his name
Take him to the cleaners and devastate him
Wipe him out, humiliate him
We don't want the whole world saying
They can't even win a game
Americans We have never reckoned
On coming second
All Delegates There's no use in losing
Americans It's the red flag up against stars and stripes
But we're peace-loving types
All Delegates No-one can deny that these are difficult times
Walter It's a sweet hail-fellow-well-met affair
For both eagle and bear

Americans These are very dangerous and difficult times
Molokov To those that say that this is not a friendly clash
Don't be so rash!
I assure you, comrades, that is balderdash
All Delegates What a load of whingeing peasants!
Thinking they can win — they can't!
What an exhibition of self-delusion
This one's a foregone conclusion
But enough of all this beating
Round the bushes of détente
Russians We intend to collar
The Yankee dollar
Americans We shall trash them
Thrash them
Molokov How good to feel that as this great event begins
It underpins
Our quest for peace, the bonds of common interest
Of East and West
Americans As long as our man wins
Russians As long as our man
All Delegates — wins!

The Arbiter enters with a Chorus of Arbiter acolytes

Song 8: "The Arbiter"

Arbiter I've a duty as the referee
At the start of the match
On behalf of all our sponsors
I must welcome you
Which I do — there's a catch

I don't care if you're a champion
No-one messes with me
I am ruthless in upholding
What I know is right
Black or white — as you'll see

I'm on the case
Can't be fooled

Any objection
Is overruled
Yes, I'm the Arbiter and I know best

Chorus He's impartial, don't push him, he's unimpressed

Arbiter You got your tricks
Good for you
But there's no gambit
I don't see through
Oh, I'm the Arbiter, I know the score

Arbiter and Chorus From square one I'll be watching all sixty-four

Arbiter If you're thinking of the kind of thing
That we've seen in the past
Chanting gurus, walkie-talkies,
Walk-outs, hypnotists,
Tempers, fists — not so fast

This is not the start of World War Three
No political ploys
I think both your constitutions are terrific so
Now you know — be good boys

I'm on the case
Can't be fooled
Any objection
Is overruled
Yes, I'm the Arbiter and I know best

Chorus He's impartial, don't push him, he's unimpressed

Arbiter You got your tricks
Good for you
But there's no gambit
I don't see through
Oh, I'm the Arbiter, I know the score

Arbiter and Chorus From square one I'll be watching all sixty-four

Arbiter I'm on the case — can't be fooled!
You got your tricks — good for you!
I'm on the case
Can't be fooled
Any objection
Is overruled
Yes, I'm the Arbiter I know best

Chorus He's impartial, don't push him, he's unimpressed

Arbiter Yes, I'm the Arbiter, I know the score

Arbiter and Chorus From square one I'll be watching all sixty-four

Florence enters to take up a central position amid the American delegation

Arbiter If the leaders of both delegations are now present, we are available to *consider* their pre-match applications, representations or objections. Miss Vassy?

Florence Thank you. The American delegation wishes to protest the size of the Soviet delegation which far exceeds the permitted number ——

Molokov Our delegation consists of just four people including our champion. Our doctor, PT expert, psychologist, security agents and chef cannot be considered delegates.

Arbiter Objection overruled. Mr Molokov?

Molokov The Soviet delegation has reason to believe that the American player's chair could contain communications devices and therefore objects to the constitution of the chair ——

Florence Both chairs were made in Sweden, with non-aligned aluminium ——

Arbiter Objection overruled.

Walter On behalf of the televison companies, making such a major financial contribution to this match, I request the Arbiter's permission for an opportunity to be given to a few commercial supporters of chess to set up a discreet display of wares in the arena ——

Molokov and Russians Objection!

Arbiter Mr de Courcey, further economic discussion with my office could clear the way to a fresh look at the status of merchandising and advertising interests — but now let us dedicate ourselves to the spirit of chess!

Song 9: "Hymn"

All Don't you find it rather touching to behold
The game that came in from the cold
Seen for what it is — religion plus finesse
Countries, classes, creeds as one in
Love of chess

Suddenly the cathedral-like atmosphere is shattered by the entrance of a garish, colourful, cheerleading mob of Merchandisers

Song 10: "The Merchandisers"

Merchandisers Whether you are pro or anti
Or could not care less
We are here to tell you
We are here to sell you chess
Not a chance of you escaping from our wiles
We've locked the doors, we've blocked the aisles
We've a franchise worth exploiting
And we will — yes, we will!
When it comes to merchandising
We could kill

When you get up —
When you get up in the morning
Till you crash at night
You will find yourself surrounded
By our copyright
Clean your teeth with chequered toothpaste
Wear our vests
Our kings and queens on bouncing breasts
You could even buy a set
And learn to play
We don't mind we'll sell you something
Anyway

We've done all our market research
And our findings show
That this game of chess could be around

A month or so
Maybe it's a bit confusing
For a game
But Rubik's Cubes were much the same
In the end the whole world bought one
All were gone
By which time we merchandisers
Had moved on

By which time we had moved on!

Scene 5

The arena

Music: Chess (instrumental)

The scene dissolves from the Arbiter's chambers to the spectacular setting for the match. The two players say nothing during this scene. However, their manner at the board becomes more and more agitated during the scene. They both get up from the board and get into a near fight, which ends with Frederick pushing Anatoly into the table, spilling board and pieces over the floor

Florence, Molokov, and Arbiter and his assistants are present. Throughout the scene commentators and commentaries on the big match are heard. At the end, there is pandemonium

TV Presenter There has been a sensational development in the very first game of the World Chess Championship here in the snow-covered Tyrolean town of Merano, Italy. The board and the pieces have been thrown to the floor in disgust by one or other or both players, the champion has walked out in a rage ...

Song 11: "The Arbiter" (reprise)

Arbiter I'm on the case
Can't be fooled
Any objection

Is overruled
Don't try to tempt me
You've no hope
I don't like women
And I don't take dope
I'm the Arbiter, my word is law

Arbiter and Chorus From square one he'll be watching you!

The Chorus and TV Presenters exit

Florence, Molokov, Anatoly and the Arbiter remain in the arena

Song 12: "A Model of Decorum and Tranquillity" (Quartet)

Molokov
We wish, no must, make our disgust
At this abuse perfectly clear
We're here for chess — are the US?
If so, why foul the atmosphere?
We wish, no must, make our disgust
At this abuse perfectly clear
We're here for chess — are the US?
How can you have such a claim?

Florence
I must protest — our delegation has a host of valid points to raise
Our player's sporting attitude's beyond all praise
As any neutral would attest
But we concede
The fact his masters bend the rules is not a player's fault
We'll overlook their crude political assault
And under protest will proceed

Arbiter
I call this tune
No-one's immune
To my power in this hall

Molokov
If your man's so sweet
Then why his fighting talk?
If he's not a cheat then why on earth
Did he go take a walk?

Florence I am not surprised he wanted fresher air
Once he realized there was no hope
Of your lot playing fair
How sad to see what used to be

Molokov Why let him loose?
He'll soon reduce
This great event to a brawl
It's very sad to see the ancient and distinguished game
That used to be

Molokov
Florence A model of decorum and tranquillity
Become like any other sport
A battleground for rival ideologies
To slug it out with glee

Anatoly I would say with regard to him,
It is hard to rebut
Ever-growing suspicions
My opposition's a nut

Molokov We wish, no must, make our disgust
At this abuse perfectly clear
We're here for chess — are the US?
If so, why foul the atmosphere?

Florence I don't suppose
You'd understand
The strain and pressure getting where he's got
For then you'd simply call him highly strung
And not imply that he was one of those

Arbiter I must insist
That you desist
If you value
Your livelihood

Anatoly But how can you
Work for one who
Treats you like dirt?
Pay must be good!

Molokov It seems to us there's little point

In waiting here all night for his return
And since a peaceful match is our sole concern
We won't make an official fuss

Florence I'm not getting rich
My only interest is
In something which gives me the chance of working with the best

Molokov In short we rise
Above your guy's
Tantrums, dramas, dirty tricks

Anatoly I can only say
I hope your dream comes true
Till that far off day
I hope you cope with helping number two

Arbiter Get this straight
I will not
Stand by
While you play at politics

Florence
Anatoly } How sad to see

Arbiter
Molokov } It's very sad to see the ancient and distinguished game
That used to be

All A model of decorum and tranquillity
Become like any other sport
A battleground for rival ideologies
To slug it out with glee

Arbiter Enough of this pious waffle! If the players do not return to the arena within twenty-four hours, the match is null and void — the game is greater than its players.

The Arbiter exits, as does Anatoly

Florence and Molokov remain to salvage the situation

Molokov The game is greater than its players, Miss Vassy — how true!

Song 13: "Florence & Molokov"

I don't know how you can allow this
Harm to be done to chess, and how this
Baby of yours can be persuaded
Back to the game

Florence Easy. You stop playing politics and start playing chess.

I don't know how you have the gall to
Criticize us when it is all too
Obvious this is what you wanted —
We get the blame

Your man, no doubt following orders, was after some sort of bust-up from the word go ——

Molokov You really are mad! He has no orders!
Now let me put my cards upon the table
If he is aggrieved then who can blame him?
He is up against a man who's less than stable

Florence Freddie less than stable? You're goading him —
Who rocked his chair throughout the match, then?
Who sniffed and coughed, began to scratch then
Played with his flag and drummed his fingers?
Then took a walk!

Your precious boy!

Molokov A piccydillo ——

Florence Peccadillo.

Molokov — peccadillo compared with the neurotic behaviour of Trumper.

Florence Listen, you Plutocratic throwback
You and your cronies want to go back
Home to your dachas, not the saltmines?

We better talk.

Molokov I wish, Florens (*he mispronounces her name*) ——

Florence Florence.

Molokov — you would refrain from cheap political jibes at a time when co-operation between us is vital. Besides, I would have thought you would be reluctant to criticize fellow Eastern Europeans.

Florence "Fellow Eastern Europeans"! I am Hungarian, remember Hungary? I wish *I* could. But I was only five when you bastards moved in. I have no memory of my homeland, my people, my mother and father — all taken from me by *you* — and you call yourself a fellow Eastern European!

Molokov Come now, Miss Vassy, we're digressing
Back to the point — let's start addressing
All our attention to the World Chess Championship

A long pause. Florence wonders whether to contemplate any further dealings with this man. She decides that she has to. She takes out a piece of paper from her handbag

Florence The Merano Mountain Inn — famous for its peace and tranquillity — that is where I want you to deliver me one Soviet Grandmaster ...

Florence refuses Molokov's handshake

Molokov exits

Florence moves into:

Scene 6

A television studio and control room

Frederick is already there with Walter

Walter For God's sake — be reasonable ——
Frederick Twenty thousand dollars!
Walter Why should we pay you to televise tantrums?
We prefer to see chess being played
(*He sees Florence as he prepares to leave*)
You can deal with him — he's getting heated —
Now he's claiming that he's underpaid!

He exits

Frederick (*into a microphone*) I said, twenty thousand dollars — a game! (*He wheels round to face Florence*) And as for you —

Song 14: "1956 — Budapest Is Rising"

I shouldn't have to be dealing with Walter
Where were you when the shit hit the fan?

Florence Saving your income by fixing a meeting
So you better start liking the man! (*She hands him a piece of paper*)

Frederick (*ignoring the paper*) When the interest is bigger than ever
And my walk-out my smartest move yet
All you say is that I ought to meet him
On the top of a mountain?

Florence You bet!

Frederick Can't you see that you're losing your grip, dear
Are the Communists fooling you, too?
Why should I be the only one trying ——

Florence You wanna lose your only friend?
Well, keep it up, you're doing fine
Why this humiliation?
Why treat me like a fool?
I've taken shit for seven years
And I won't take it anymore

Frederick I'm only teasing Soviets
With gentle bonhomie
And you've a better reason to be anti-them than me

Florence There's a time and there's a place

Frederick Well, how about here and now? Are you for me or for them?

Florence There's a time and there's a place

Frederick (*into a microphone; his voice is duplicated and reprocessed*)
Nineteen fifty-six — Budapest is rising
Nineteen fifty-six — Budapest is fighting
I'd have thought you'd support
Any attack on these people
On the people who ran
Mindlessly over your childhood
Don't let them fool you for
Thirty years on they're the same

Florence Nineteen fifty-six — Budapest is falling
Nineteen fifty-six — Budapest is dying

Frederick They see chess as a war
Playing with pawns just like Poland
If you walk out on me

They've got you like they got your father
Were he alive now he'd surely be dying of shame

Florence You know that there's nothing I've done
That he'd be ashamed of in my whole life!
Why'd you have to do this to me?

Frederick exits

Song 15: "Nobody's Side"

What's going on around me
Is barely making sense
I need some explanations fast
I see my present partner
In the imperfect tense
And I don't see how we can last
I feel I need a change of cast
Maybe I'm on nobody's side

And when he gives me reasons
To justify each move
They're getting harder to believe
I know this can't continue
I've still a lot to prove
There must be more I could achieve
But I don't have the nerve to leave

Everybody's playing the game
But nobody's rules are the same
Nobody's on nobody's side
Better learn to go it alone
Recognize you're out on your own
Nobody's on nobody's side

The one I should not think of
Keeps rolling through my mind
And I don't want to let that go
No lover ever faithful
No contract truly signed
There's nothing certain left to know

And how the cracks begin to show

Never make a promise or plan
Take a little love where you can
Nobody's on nobody's side
Never stay too long in your bed
Never lose your heart, use your head
Nobody's on nobody's side

Never take a stranger's advice
Never let a friend fool you twice
Nobody's on nobody's side
Never be the first to believe
Never be the last to deceive
Nobody's on nobody's side

Never leave a moment too soon
Never waste a hot afternoon
Nobody's on nobody's side
Never stay a minute too long
Don't forget the best will go wrong
Nobody's on nobody's side

You'd better learn to go it all alone
Recognize you're out on your own
Nobody's on nobody's side

The set changes to the Merano Mountain Inn. Florence puts on a coat

OK — now for the Merano Mountain Inn.

Scene 7

A restaurant halfway up a mountain in Merano. It is packed with laughing, noisy, celebrating people, many singing the drinking song "Der Kleine Franz". *Anatoly is in the middle of the crowd*

Florence enters and fights her way through to Anatoly. They try to talk but it's impossible. They decide to go outside

Song 16: "*Der Kleine Franz*"

Chorus

Der Kleine Franz
Er sagt: ein prosit
Meide den Schmerz!
Ich bin wie ein
Tannenbaum so grün im Herz
Bier ist was ich brauche
Wann im Hofbrauhaus
Trinken Brüderlein,
Und lassen die Sorgen aus
Es gibt gemütlichkeit
Und Freude, saubere zunft
Lorelei und Bratwurst
Gute Nacht zukunft!
Und jetzt
Im tiefen Keller
Sitz ich hier
Schon am Morgen
Fing' ich an
Und trinke Bier

Der Kleine Franz
Ist auf der Heide
Ich bin im Wald
Lustig bin ich nicht
Mein Sauerkraut ist kalt!
Drunten in dem grünen Thal
Ein Birnbaum steht
Lieben bringt uns
Grosse Freud' und Zeit
Bald vergeht
Er war in Heidelberg gesoffen
Ein braver Mann!
Hier in München
Niemand das Vertragen kann
Zum wohl!
Da streiten sich
Die Leut' herum
Brüderlein und Kummer
Sind ja nicht so dumm

Outside, away from the noise:

Song 17: "Mountain Duet"

Florence This is the one situation
I wanted most to avoid
Nothing I say will convince him it isn't a trick

Anatoly A drink on a clear moonlit night — I relax, she smiles
There's something peculiar going on

Florence So, through my own stupid fault I'm stuck here to carry the can
Embarrassed, deserted, marooned

Anatoly Now she can't be working for them — I mean us —
She seems so very straightforward — but where is *he*?

Florence He has to turn up — it's not just the money — perhaps it is!

Anatoly Maybe he's scared — just as scared as he was in the game

Florence Oh, I just couldn't care less
He can go right ahead, go and wreck his career,
I know I've done my best

Anatoly Well, at least she's a good-looking spy

Florence What if our Russian friend thinks that my plans
Have nothing to do with the chess?
If I don't say something else soon
He'll go — Nobody's on nobody's side!

Anatoly (*for the first time addressing Florence*) Listen, I hate to break up the mood
Get to the point, begin the beguine
Haven't you noticed we are one character short
In this idyllic, well-produced scene?

Florence He couldn't wait to join you up here
Maybe he walked, cable-cars scare him

Anatoly Never mind him — I haven't missed him so far

Florence Maybe it won't do any harm
To struggle on without his charm

Anatoly Funny how at all once I feel that he can go jump off the mountain, I won't care

Florence This is the one situation I wanted most to avoid

Anatoly My dear opponent — I really can't imagine why
Florence So I am not dangerous then? What a shame!
Anatoly Oh, you're not dangerous — who could think that of you?
Florence You — you are so strange — why can't you be what you ought to be?
You should be scheming, intriguing, too clever by half —
Anatoly I have to hand it to you
For you managed to make me forget why I ever agreed
to this farce
Both I don't know why I can't think of anything
I would rather do
Than be wasting my time on mountains with you

They are suddenly aware that they have been joined by Frederick

Frederick Who'd ever think it?
Such a very pretty setting
Tell me what's the betting
Very pretty plotting too?
No matter — I've done all your work for you

(*To Florence*) What do all Soviets deserve? Have you forgotten? Well, you'll soon remember!

Who'd ever guess it?
Daughter in collaboration
With the very nation
Gave the father third degree!
Where's Daddy? Dead, or in the KGB?

Florence runs off

I have agreed new terms which, in short, means more money. For you as well, but that can't be helped. This meeting is therefore unnecessary — the match can continue and we don't have to be friends.

Anatoly and Frederick are left staring at each other. They are already in their positions for the continuation of the match

Scene 8

The arena and surrounding areas

Music: Chess (instrumental). The match has been resumed. We see it through the eyes of the world's media. Anatoly forges ahead to a 5-1 lead

Scene 9

Frederick/Florence's suite. Frederick is there already

Florence enters

Frederick Five games to one! It's all over —

Song 18: "Florence Quits"

So you got what you want
What a nasty ambition!
Set me up, pull me down
Then exploit my condition
I should have guessed, woman,
That if pressed, woman,
You're on nobody's side but your own
And you're behaving
Like a mere woman
It's so clear, woman —
It's your sex!
Once they start getting old and getting worried
They let fly, take it out
On the one who supports them
That's you I'm talking about

Florence Who'd ever think it?
Such a squalid little ending
Watching you descending
Just as far as you can go
I'm learning things I didn't want to know

Frederick Who'd ever guess it?
This would be the situation —

One more observation —
How'd we ever get this far
Before you showed me what you really are?

Florence You'll be lost without me
To abuse like you used to

She exits

Frederick Go away! Just get out! Be someone else's parasite!

But Florence has already gone

Song 19: "Pity the Child"

When I was nine I learned survival
Taught myself not to care
I was my single good companion
Taking my comfort there
Up in my room I planned my conquests
On my own, never asked for a helping hand
No-one would understand
I never asked the pair who fought below
Just in case they said no

Pity the child who has ambition
Knows what he wants to do
Knows that he'll never fit the system
Others expect him to
Pity the child who knew his parents
Saw their faults, saw their love die before his eyes
Pity the child that wise
He never asked, did I cause your distress?
Just in case they said yes

When I was twelve my father moved out
Left with a whimper not with a shout
I didn't miss him he made it perfectly clear
I was a fool and probably queer
Fool that I was I thought this would bring
Those he had left closer together

She made her move the moment he crawled away
I was the last the woman told
She never let her bed get cold
Someone moved in — I shut my door
Someone to treat her just the same way as before

I took the road of least resistance
I had my game to play
I had the skill, and more — the hunger
Easy to get away
Pity the child with no such weapons
No defence, no escape from the ties that bind
Always a step behind
I never called to tell her all I'd done
I was only her son!

Pity the child but not forever
Not if he stays that way
He can get all he ever wanted
If he's prepared to pay
Pity instead the careless mother
What she missed
What she lost when she let me go
And I wonder does she know
I wouldn't call — a crazy thing to do —
Just in case she said who?

Back in the Arbiter's chambers the Arbiter opens an envelope before an anxious gathering of all those involved in the championship

Arbiter Frederick Trumper has resigned. Anatoly Sergievsky is the new World Champion.

Sensation. Wild celebrations and back-slapping in the Russian camp. Florence is alone and still on her side of the stage. Suddenly, Anatoly breaks free of his colleagues and runs to Florence

They both rush off

TV Presenter The drama at the World Chess Championship here in Merano, Italy, is now off the board. Barely had Anatoly Sergievsky of the Soviet Union been proclaimed the new World Champion thanks to his crushing of former champion Freddie Trumper of the United States, when he upstaged his own triumph by deserting his Soviet team and supporters. He is believed to be seeking political asylum in the West ...

Scene 10

An unspecified embassy or, more likely, a consulate in Merano

Walter leads Anatoly and Florence into the consulate. Civil Servants seem uninterested

Song 20: "Embassy Lament"

Civil Servants (*to each other*) Oh my dear, how boring
He's defecting
Just like all the others he's expecting
Us to be impressed with what he's done here
But he
Hasn't stopped to think about the paperwork
His gesture causes
We've an embassy to run here!
If these people can't strike blows for freedom
With a valid visa
We don't need 'em

(*To Anatoly*) If we seem offhand then please remember
This is nothing very special
You're the fourth we've had since last November

(*To each other*) Who do these foreign chappies think they are?
And when he's safely in the West
He'll be the hero to discuss
The media will lionise him
Fame and fortune plus
No-one will recall
It's thanks to us

Civil Servant 1 You have a wife?
Anatoly Yes.
Civil Servant 1 You have two children?
Anatoly Yes.
Civil Servant 2 And they are not coming with you?

Florence and Walter both show particular but differing interest in this conversation. Maybe Walter scribbles something on a pad

Anatoly No — not for the moment.
Civil Servant 2 You play chess. You are good at it? Ah yes, it says here you are World Champion.
Anatoly Since yesterday.
Civil Servant 1 That's still good.
Walter Gentlemen, you guys are dealing with a major international figure! May I ——
Civil Servant 2 Are you defecting too, sir?
Walter No. This man is a citizen of the Soviet Union — I am an American citizen, and by the authority of this government and this agency (*he shows the Civil Servants a card*), I demand that you give this man your immediate attention.
Civil Servants Have you an appointment with the consul?
If you don't we know what his response'll
Be, he will not see you, with respect it
Buggers up his very taxing schedule
Pushing peace and understanding
Let us hope this won't affect it
Far too many jokers cross the border
Not a single document in order
Russia must be empty, though we're all for
Basic human rights, it makes you wonder
What they built the Berlin Wall for
Who do these foreign chappies think they are?
And when you've filled in all the forms
And been passed clear of all disease
Debriefed, debugged, dedrugged, disarmed
And disinfected, please
Don't forget the guys who cut your keys

As the paperwork staggers on, Florence moves away from the argument

Song 21: "Heaven Help My Heart"

Florence

If it were love I would give that love every second I had
And I do
Did I know where he'll lead me to?
Did I plan
Doing all of this for the love of a man?
Well, I let it happen anyhow
And what I'm feeling now
Has no easy explanation, reason plays no part
Heaven help my heart
I love him too much
What if he saw my whole existence
Turning around a word, a smile, a touch?

One of these days, and it won't be long, he'll know more about me
Than he should
All my dreams will be understood
No surprise
Nothing more to learn from the look in my eyes
Though I know that time is not my friend
I'll fight it to the end
Hoping to keep that best of moments
When the passions start
Heaven help my heart
The day that I find
Suddenly I've run out of secrets
Suddenly I'm not always on his mind

Maybe it's best to love a stranger
Well, that's what I've done — Heaven help my heart
Heaven help my heart

Various documents are stamped and handed to Anatoly

With great delight he rushes over to Florence and they hurry out

Walter picks up a phone

Scene 11

Walter, Florence and Anatoly arrive at Merano station. As they arrive they are surrounded by pressmen

Reporter 1 Excuse me, Mr Sergievsky, why are you leaving Russia?

Anatoly tries to brush him off

What about your wife and family?

Song 22: "Anatoly and the Press"

Reporters
How long was this planned?
What made you defect?
Did anyone help you?
And do you expect
To be joined in your exile
By loved ones, e.g. your wife?
Or are you starting again
In all aspects of life?

Anatoly (*to Walter*) You bastard! You never told me you'd fixed all this!
Reporter 2 Why did you leave Russia?
Anatoly I don't *leave* anything.

Song 23: "Anthem"

No man, no madness
Though their sad power may prevail
Can possess, conquer, my country's heart
They rise to fail
She is eternal
Long before nations' lines were drawn
When no flags flew, when no armies stood
My land was born

And you ask me why I love her
Through wars, death and despair
She is the constant, we who don't care

And you wonder will I leave her — but how?
I cross over borders but I'm still there now

How can I leave her?
Where would I start?
Let man's petty nations tear themselves apart
My land's only border lies around my heart

CURTAIN

ACT II
Scene 1

The streets of Bangkok, a year later

The scene opens with a ballet (Music 24: "The Golden Bangkok") leading into "One Night in Bangkok"

The match (Anatoly v. Leonid Viigand, the new Soviet Champion) has already started as Frederick argues with the locals in the song

Song 25: "One Night in Bangkok"

Frederick

Bangkok! Oriental setting
And the city don't know what the city is getting
The *crème de la crème* of the chess world in a
Show with everything but Yul Brynner

Time flies! Doesn't seem a minute
Since a Tyrolean spa had the chess boys in it
All change! Don't you know that when you
Play at this level there's no ordinary venue
It's Iceland — or the Philippines — or Hastings — or —
or this place!

Chorus

One night in Bangkok and the world's your oyster
The bars are temples but the pearls ain't free
You'll find a god in every golden cloister
And if you're lucky then the god's a she
I can feel an angel sliding up to me

Frederick

One town's very like another
When your head's down over your pieces, brother

Chorus

It's a drag, it's a bore, it's really such a pity
To be looking at the board, not looking at the city

Frederick Whaddaya mean? You've seen one crowded, polluted, stinking town ——

Chorus Tea, girls, warm, sweet
Some are set up in the Somerset Maugham suite

Frederick Get Thai'd! You're talking to a tourist
Whose every move's among the purest
I get my kicks above the waistline, sunshine

Chorus One night in Bangkok makes a hard man humble
Not much between despair and ecstasy
One night in Bangkok and the tough guys tumble
Can't be too careful with your company
I can feel the devil walking next to me

Frederick Siam's gonna be the witness
To the ultimate test of cerebral fitness
This grips me more than would a
Muddy old river or reclining Buddha
And thank God I'm only watching the game — controlling it —
I don't see you guys rating
The kind of mate I'm contemplating
I'd let you watch, I would invite you
But the queens we use would not excite you
So you'd better go back to your bars, your temples, your massage parlours

Chorus One night in Bangkok and the world's your oyster
The bars are temples but the pearls ain't free
You'll find a god in every golden cloister
A little flesh, a little history
I can feel an angel sliding up to me

One night in Bangkok makes a hard man humble
Not much between despair and ecstasy
One night in Bangkok and the tough guys tumble
Can't be too careful with your company
I can feel the devil walking next to me

Scene 2

The Oriental Hotel, Bangkok

Anatoly and Florence are in their suite. They are watching Frederick on television

Frederick (*on television*) This is Frederick Trumper on behalf of International Global Television. The all-Russian struggle for world chess supremacy is well under way here in steamy Bangkok, Thailand. But it's also a titanic battle between East and West, with the current World Champion a stateless person, having defected to the free world when he won his title last year in icy Merano, Italy.

Anatoly changes channels, gets Abba singing "Money Money Money", and switches back to Frederick

It's honours even so far with the match only two games old. In the first game Sergievsky was inspired and Viigand played like a man petrified, awestruck ——

Song 26: "One More Opponent"

Anatoly (*switching off the television*) But why is he really here?
A whole year of silence
Then suddenly here he is —
Florence He's working for the TV company, for a *lot* of money.
Anatoly So that's all it is then?
He has no desire to see you anymore?
Florence Who cares what he's up to?
You're not playing him
Anatoly Oh no? I've the feeling I am
Why is he here?
Florence Don't talk yourself out of form
Viigand's the one
You have to beat
Anatoly And he's a fine player
Florence Predictable — he's a machine!
Anatoly A very fine machine!

Florence (*light-heartedly, affectionately*) So are you — so are we!
Um, there is one other thing

Anatoly What?

Florence I gather Svetlana is hoping to come out here

Anatoly My wife? Come to Bangkok?

Florence You must know about it.
It's been in the paper
They may let her out ——

Anatoly This has to be Molokov — right up his street!

Florence So now you've got one more opponent to beat
Surely you knew ——

Anatoly (*angrily*) I did not!

Pause

Florence Well, this is a problem we knew we'd be facing soon

Anatoly But not now. But not now.

Song 27: "You and I"

Florence This is an all too familiar scene

Anatoly Life imperceptibly coming between

Both Those whose love is as strong
As it could or should be
Nothing has altered
Yet everything's changed
No-one stands still
Still I love you completely and hope I always will
Each day we get through means one less mistake left for the making

Anatoly And there's no return
As we slowly learn
Of the chance we're taking

Florence I'd give the world to stay just as we are
It's better by far
Not to be too wise

Both Not to realize
Where there's truth there will be lies

Florence You and I
We've seen it all
Been down this road before
Yet we go on believing ——

Both You and I
We've seen it all
Chasing our heart's desire
Yet I'm even more certain
This time it will be
My happy ending

The telephone rings. Anatoly answers it

Anatoly (*into the phone*) Thank you. (*He hangs up*) The car to take me to the television studio is here. You know, the interview I promised Walter ——

Florence Fine — ask Walter what *he* knows. Maybe they've fixed the result of the match already. We could go home now if you're going to lose.

Anatoly exits

Scene 3

Molokov's hotel suite

Molokov and his cronies have assembled at their headquarters in their Bangkok hotel. Throughout this scene only Viigand, Anatoly's challenger, seems interested in chess: he pores over a board, making moves for both black and white, ignoring most of the discussion around him. They have been bugging Anatoly and Florence. We hear their last speeches from the previous scene over again

Molokov Comrades — why are you looking so worried? We're not dealing with the traitor Sergievsky now. Comrade Viigand here is a disciplined Soviet chess-playing machine!

Song 28: "The Soviet Machine"

Just in case you feel a trace
Of doubt or even nervous tension
Let me draw the latest score
To your attention

Not the score the witless corps
Of commentators are debating
Come, admit — who gives a shit
For Elo rating?

No, I prefer and I'm sure you concur
To see who's ahead
Psychologically
For example:

We have on tap an inscrutable chap
Whose thoughts never stray
From the state of the play

He bangs a gong in Viigand's ear. No response

Fantastic! Whereas ——

It's so difficult to concentrate if
You have left your native
Country for a woman who has plans of her own
It's not easy for a chap to excel
Feeling guilty as hell
Having left his wife to face the music alone

But even worse, imagine if his ladies met
Well, then I bet
The atmosphere round here would be a little strained
As he explained
How he could do what he's done to those two
Most wonderful girls
"Yes, I love you both!"

Cronies Most amusing!
Molokov Starting from scratch they'll torpedo his match
His horse-power dead
On the board and in bed
Molokov Bit by bit the pieces fit
Cronies The Soviet machine advances
Not one move that won't improve
Our nation's chances

We predict a stunning victory
Both on the board and off it
This will show the traitor
No-one rats with profit

Oh, we're gonna smash that bastard!
Make him wanna change his name
Take him to the cleaners and devastate him
Wipe him out, humiliate him
We don't want the whole world saying
They can't even win a game
We have never reckoned on coming second
There's no use in losing

Cronies We can feel the flame of triumph burning
Our people's pride returning
Molokov } Not one move that won't improve
Cronies } Our nation's chances

They raise their glasses and shout, "Hoy!"

No, I prefer and I'm sure you concur
To see who's ahead
Psychologically
For example:

We have on tap an inscrutable chap
Whose thoughts never stray
From the state of the play

La la la ...

Bit by bit the pieces fit
The Soviet machine advances
Not one move that won't improve
Our nation's chances

Hey! Hey!

We predict a stunning victory
Both on the board and off it
This will show the traitor
No-one rats with profit

La la la ... La!

From Moscow to the Bering Straits
Citizens will hail our victory
In Arctic circles frozen states
Will join with warmer climes in revelry
And I can say of this affair
I was there, did my share, played my part
And Russians all will be aware
I was there, from the start
Mmm — mmm

Viigand Checkmate! Good-night.

They are all asleep or drunk or both, save Molokov and a Waiter. Molokov goes to the telephone and makes a call

Molokov (*into the telephone*) Mr de Courcey?... Good news. We are going to be able to help each other. ... Yes, heartwarming international co-operation. I have the proof that Florence Vassy's father is alive. ... You are going to be able to stage a great human rights victory and all we want is a tiny triumph on the chess board. ... It's on its way to you now. ... What's that?... Thank *you*, Walter. ... Goodbye. (*He hangs up and hands an envelope to the Waiter*)

The Waiter takes the envelope to Walter as the scene dissolves into the next — a TV studio

Scene 4

A television studio. Walter reads the letter. He registers astonishment

Frederick arrives

Song 29: "Interview"

Walter Remember last night I was saying
The interview shouldn't be vicious?

Frederick looks surprised

Well, times have moved on and
Forget what I told you
You have my permission, no — order
To go for the jugular — just as you wanted

Frederick Well, that's fine by me, but why the change?

Walter It seems to me on reflection
We don't need to pander to Russians
He may have defected
He may be a good guy
But face it, he's yesterday's issue
Here are some questions — go for him! (*He hands Frederick a sheet of questions*)

Frederick exits to get ready for the programme

(*To the Floor Manager*) Whatever, and I mean whatever,
They say or do make sure you stay on the Russian
Don't let your cameras off him for a moment, and get the Svetlana video lined up!
Is this the tide in my affairs
When I write a little history?
Or just an interview whose wares
Will flood the screens with triviality?

Anatoly arrives

Walter greets him with exaggerated warmth

Ah, Anatoly! If I may,
Let me say right away
You'll be thrilled
Because the other seat is filled
By a long-standing friend
Of yours!

Frederick returns

Anatoly is amazed and angry when he sees who is to interview him. Walter steers them both on to the same studio sofa before Anatoly has time to protest. The cameras spring into life — they are on the air

TV Presenter Tonight's final item is a fascinating confrontation in connection with the World Chess Championship. The former World Champion talks to the man who took his title a year ago in Merano, Italy, and who is defending that title right now here in Bangkok.

Frederick Well, here we are face to face once again
Anatoly By any standards a bizarre reunion
Frederick Is being homeless affecting your game?
Anatoly I wouldn't know, since I've a home in England
Frederick No, by a home I mean real home — the place where your family is
Anatoly England is my real home!
Frederick What are your latest political aims?
Anatoly What are you saying?
Frederick Your anti-Russian crusade — has it worked?
Anatoly I'm no crusader ——
Frederick What is your true motivation? That's something we all want to know
Anatoly Listen — you know damn well what my motivation is ——
Frederick (*into the camera*) Here we see a man under great pressure
Two fights to fight yet he could not look fresher
Chess and politics! I take my hat off
To any champion who can pull that off
I hear your second controls everything

Anatoly Chess is her passion
Frederick But her obsession is East versus West
Anatoly *Chess* is her passion
Frederick I know a little about her and she's got her own axe to grind
Anatoly That's not true ——
Frederick Aren't you concerned that your wife's not here?
Anatoly I don't discuss my private life in public ——
Frederick But don't you care that she's not by your side?
Anatoly I think I've had enough of this discussion ——
Frederick Well, we've a little surprise, we have your wife on the video —
Let her talk to you, give you her version
How married life has changed since your desertion
Hey! Come back, my friend, we're only showing
Home movies, nothing more — where are you going?

A video clip of Svetlana starts rolling. She is appealing to her husband in Russian. Anatoly pulls off his clip-on microphone (with difficulty) and attempts to leave the set

Walter (*to Anatoly*) A wonderful interview!

Anatoly barges Walter aside and exits

The video clip changes to the arrival of Svetlana at Bangkok airport

Scene 5

The foyer of the Oriental Hotel, which becomes a chessboard

The entire company is on stage

Song 30: "The Deal"

Arbiter Isn't it strange the complications
People attach to situations
Almost as if they want to miss
The wood for the trees

Nothing will change my basic feeling
When they've done all their wheeler-dealing
Those in the strongest situations
Do as they please

You might see all kinds of human emotion here — passion and pain, love and hate —

I see nothing other than a simple board game

In the Dusit Thani hotel, Bangkok, Alexander Molokov makes his first move.

Molokov (*to Svetlana*) We did not bring you to Bangkok for a holiday, my dear. You have to tell your husband that he has to lose. Talk to Anatoly, my dear!

You can have the life you want
And anywhere you want it —

But if he's going to win, then you're not going anywhere!

Make him think of you not
Narcissistic dreams of glory

How many times does he want to be champion, anyway?

Arbiter Two days later the wife makes her move ...

Svetlana How many times do you want to be champion, anyway?

Who needs a dream? Who needs ambition?
Who'd be the fool in my position?
Once I had dreams —

Anatoly Now they're obsessions
Hopes became needs, lovers possessions

Svetlana Now you're where you want to be and who you want to be
And doing what you always said you would
And yet you know you haven't won at all
Running for your life and never looking back
In case there's someone right behind to
Shoot you down and say he always knew you'd fall

When the crazy wheel slows down
Where will you be? Back where you started?

Arbiter Back at the Oriental, Walter de Courcey makes his gambit perfectly clear.

Walter (*handing a document to Florence*) Your father is alive.

Florence My father? Alive?
Walter Alive in Russia. Thirty years in prison.
Florence And you think I believe you?
Walter The evidence is conclusive. And Anatoly will believe me. Now you get Anatoly to lose to Viigand and Molokov assures me we can get your father out — and not only him ...

We have some people to recover
I know that you would simply love a
Chance to make sure your father's name
Is high on our list
We want him back which is to say a
Gesture is needed from your player
We wouldn't mind if he got beaten
In fact we insist

Florence
There must be a lie
You wouldn't tell me
A limit to your devious ambition
But what it can be
I can't imagine
Is there no-one here who's not a politician?

There's no deal! (*She hands the document back to Walter*)

Walter sidles away

When I was young I learned that memories
Shouldn't be built to last
Luxuries such as father, mother
Jettisoned in the past
How can a half-remembered figure
From a past so remote that it's hardly real
Alter the way I feel?
Pity the child who thirty-five years on
Finds that confidence gone

Arbiter While in subterranean marble surroundings two of the most powerful players make a mid-game assessment ...

Walter
You should have seen how she reacted
I couldn't leave till she'd extracted
Promises she would see her father
Simple, I said

Told her the way she could achieve this
Even though you might not believe this
She said I that I was not to worry
Go right ahead

Molokov You don't know her well
She could have fooled you
She could despite herself try to resist us

Walter Yes, maybe I'm wrong
But to be certain
There are others we can call in to assist us ...
(*He moves over to Frederick*)

Arbiter And who better than the dethroned king?

Walter Remember, Freddie, who's paying for you to be here in Bangkok — not the Chess Federation. Now we've got a deal to get some people out — including Florence's father — provided Anatoly loses, so convince him!

Frederick (*on the phone to Anatoly*) Communist, Democrat

Anatoly An intriguing collusion

Frederick Fair exchange — tit for tat

Anatoly Comradeship in profusion

Frederick And the appeal, partner
Of this deal, partner
Is we all stand to win
You and me, the lady also
Don't break her heart, partner

Frederick, Walter, Molokov Partner!

Frederick Just be smart, partner

Frederick, Walter, Molokov Partner!

Frederick Throw the game, show your love
Is as pure as snow in Moscow

Anatoly Who put you up to this? There's no deal!

Arbiter So Frederick makes a desperate final play for the woman he hasn't seen for a year.

Frederick Silly boy, woman who
I should not have let walk out

There's no hitch
That we two
Can't untangle or talk about
And the appeal, partner
Of this deal, partner
Is we both stand to win
We'll bring back the golden era
Stick with me, honey
Leave him be, honey
You don't know what they've planned
For you long ago in Moscow

Florence Can't you see we've moved on? Chess has nothing to do with this — Freddie — chess isn't life!

Frederick But I've changed — I've grown up! He won't help you! He won't throw the match! I'm telling you the truth, Florence!

Florence
Anatoly } Who'd ever think it?
Such a squalid little ending
Watching him descending
Just as far as he can go
I'm learning things I didn't want to know

Anatoly Let him spill out his hate
Till he knows he's deserted
There's no point wasting time
Preaching to the perverted

Florence
Anatoly
Frederick
Svetlana } Who'd ever guess it?
No-one makes the moves intended
Till the game is ended
Then they say I told you so
I'm learning things I didn't want to know

Frederick It can all be different now, Florence — I love you!

Arbiter Everybody's playing the game
But nobody's rules are the same

All Nobody's on nobody's side
Everybody's playing the game
But nobody's rules are the same
Nobody's on nobody's side

The men exit after The Deal

Florence and Svetlana remain. They are not aware of each other

Song 31: "I Know Him So Well"

Florence Nothing is so good it lasts eternally
Perfect situations must go wrong
But this has never yet prevented me
Wanting far too much for far too long
Looking back I could have played it differently
Won a few more moments, who can tell?
But it took time to understand the man
Now at least I know I know him well

Wasn't it good?
Svetlana Oh, so good
Florence Wasn't he fine?
Svetlana Oh, so fine
Florence Isn't it madness
Both He can't be mine?
Florence But in the end he needs a little bit more than me
More security
Svetlana He needs his fantasy and freedom
Florence I know him so well

Svetlana No-one in your life is with you constantly
No-one is completely on your side
And though I move my world to be with him
Still the gap between us is too wide
Looking back I could have played it differently
Learned about the man before I fell
But I was ever so much younger then
Florence Looking back I could have played things some other way
I was just a little careless maybe
Both Now at least I know I know him well

Svetlana Wasn't it good?
Florence Oh, so good
Svetlana Wasn't he fine?
Florence Oh, so fine

Svetlana	Isn't it madness
Both	He won't be mine?
	Didn't I know
	How it would go?
	If I knew from the start
	Why am I falling apart?
Svetlana	Wasn't it good?
	Wasn't he fine?
Florence	Isn't it madness
Both	He won't be mine?
Florence	But in the end he needs a little bit more than me —
	More security
Svetlana	He needs his fantasy and freedom
Florence	I know him so well
Svetlana	It took time to understand him
Both	I know him so well

Scene 6

A Buddhist temple

Monks are heard chanting as Anatoly enters

Anatoly (*reading from a note*) "Meet me in the temple of the Reclining Buddha"? Meet who?

Frederick enters

Oh, it's you!

Song 32: "Talking Chess"

Frederick	This is the one situation
	I wanted most to avoid ——
Anatoly	Then what on earth are we doing?
	I could be better employed ——
Frederick	No — please hear me out
	I think I can help ——
Anatoly	If it's about Florence
	I'm warning you ——

Frederick No — it's not about her, your wife, or your kids,
Or money, or Walter, or Molokov
Anatoly What the hell is it?
Frederick I want to talk chess!
Anatoly Chess?
Frederick Something I've noticed in Viigand
It's his King's Indian defence —
One of the lines he's been trying
Doesn't completely make sense ——
Anatoly I — I don't understand ——
Frederick I told you — his King's ——
Anatoly No — I don't understand why
You're helping me
Frederick Because I love chess!
Does nobody else?
Geez — sometimes I think I'm the only one
How can you let mediocrity win?
Anatoly I think I believe you. Show me.

Frederick begins to explain with a pocket chess set

Frederick You know, in all my dealings with Florence I never once made a good move.
Anatoly Me too. Freddie, if I win, it's bad for her father and I can't lose for the wrong reasons ——
Frederick How can you let mediocrity win?

Frederick exits

Scene 7

The arena. The final game in the final match between Anatoly and Viigand

Song 33: "Endgame"

Chorus Tal, Tal, Lasker, Steinitz, Steinitz, Alekhine, Borvinnik,
Smyslov, Spassky, Euwe, Karpov, Fischer, Petrosian,
Anderson, Capablanca, Capablanca, Kasparov, Morphy,
Capablanca

Arbiter Two weeks ago I gave you a limit of six more games to end this sequence of draws. Five of these have now passed. If today's game does not produce a decision, the match is void.

Frederick (*on the TV screen*) All eyes in the world of chess and indeed many eyes outside it are turned towards Bangkok, Thailand, today where the final match in this gripping encounter has just been launched with ceremonial splendour. And all the talk is of the recent and sensational loss of form of the World Champion who seems certain to surrender his title here today.

Chorus Eighteen sixty-six — Wilhelm Steinitz
Eighteen ninety-four — Emmanuel Lasker
Nineteen twenty-one — José Capablanca
Nineteen twenty-seven — Alex Alekhine
Nineteen thirty-five — Max Euwe
Nineteen forty-eight — Mikhail Botvinnik
Nineteen fifty-seven — Vasily Smyslov
Nineteen sixty — Michaël Tal
Nineteen sixty-three — Tigran Petrosian
Nineteen sixty-nine — Boris Spassky
Nineteen seventy-two — Bobby Fischer
Nineteen seventy-five — Anatoly Karpov
Nineteen eighty-five — Garry Kasparov

Molokov How straightforward the game
When one has trust in one's player
And how great the relief
Working for one who believes in
Loyalty, heritage, true to his kind come what may

Walter (*to Molokov*) Though it gives me no joy
Adding to your satisfaction
You can safely assume
Your late unlamented employee
Knows if he wins then the only thing won is the chess

Molokov It's the weak who accept
Tawdry untruths about freedom
Prostituting themselves
Chasing a spurious starlight
Trinkets in airports sufficient to lead them astray

Florence Does the player exist
In any human endeavour

Who's been known to resist
Sirens of fame and possessions?
They will destroy you, not rivals, not age, not success

Chorus

Nineteen fifty-six — Budapest is rising
Nineteen fifty-six — Budapest is fighting
Nineteen fifty-six — Budapest is falling
Nineteen fifty-six — Budapest is dying

Anatoly

They all think they see a man
Who doesn't know
Which move to make
Which way to go
Whose private life
Caused his decline
Wrecked his grand design
Some are vicious, some are fools
And others blind
To see in me
One of their kind

Anyone can be
A husband, lover
Sooner them than me
When they discover
Their domestic bliss is
Shelter for their failing

Nothing could be worse
Than self-denial
Having to rehearse
The endless trial
Of a partner's rather sad
Demands prevailing

Svetlana

As you watch yourself caring
About a minor sporting triumph, sharing
Your win with esoterics,
Paranoids, hysterics

Who don't pay attention to
What goes on around them
They leave the ones they love the way they found them
A normal person must
Dismiss you with disgust
And weep for those who trusted you

Anatoly Nothing you have said
Is revelation
Take my blues as read
My consolation —
Finding out at last my one true obligation!

Florence Since you seem to have shut out
The world at large then maybe I should cut out
My tiny inessential
World, inconsequential
In the kind of games you're playing
How do you do it?
I tried to be that cynical but blew it
I only changed your life
You left your home, your wife,
I'm not surprised I slipped your mind

Anatoly Nothing you have said
Is revelation
Take my blues as read
My consolation —
Finding out at last my one true obligation!

Svetlana, Florence, Chorus Listen to them shout!
They saw you do it
In their minds no doubt
That you've been through it
Suffered for your art but
In the end a winner

We have never heard
Such an ovation
Who could not be stirred?
Such dedication
Skill and guts a model
For the young beginner

They're completely enchanted
But they don't take your qualities for granted
It isn't very often
That the critics soften
Nonetheless you've won their hearts
How can we begin to
Appreciate the work that you've put into
Your calling through the years
The blood, sweat and tears
The late, late nights, the early starts
There they go again!
Your deeds inflame them
Drive them wild, but then
Who wants to tame them?
If they want a part of you
Who'd really blame them?

Anatoly And so you're letting me know ——

Florence For you're the only one who's never suffered anything at all

Anatoly How you've hated my success ——

Svetlana Well, I won't crawl —
And you can slink back to your pawns and to your tarts

Anatoly And every poisoned word shows that you never understood

Svetlana Liar!

Anatoly Never!

Svetlana Liar!

Anatoly Never!

Florence Liar!

Anatoly Never!

Svetlana, Florence Liar!

Anatoly Never! Never!

Anatoly, Svetlana, Florence Nothing you have said
Is revelation
Take my blues as read
My consolation ——

Svetlana, Florence Finding out that I'm my only obligation

Anatoly Is there no-one in my life

Who does not claim
The right to steal
My work, my name
My success, my fame
And my freedom?

As Anatoly concludes his words, he sets off on a series of sensational moves that culminate in the checkmate of Viigand. Pandemonium ensues

Arbiter Anatoly Sergievsky is the winner.

Scene 8

The arena after all the crowds have gone

Florence So — you've done it! You're still the champion.
Anatoly I had to win. If I had lost for Molokov, I would be the same as Molokov. I had to win to be free.
Florence Free? For what?
Anatoly Free to decide what we are going to do.
Florence No, Anatoly. You aren't free ... neither am I. You have to go back — your wife and your family ——
Anatoly Your father ——

Song 34a: "You and I" (reprise)

Florence This is an all too familiar scene
Anatoly Life imperceptibly coming between
Both Those whose love is as strong as it could or should be
Florence I'd give the world to stay just as we are
It's better by far
Both Not to be too wise
As we realize
There was truth and there were lies

The arena dissolves into the airport

Anatoly Knowing I want you
Knowing I love you

Why I remain
Careless about you

Florence I've been a fool to allow
Dreams to become great expectations

Anatoly How can I love you so much yet make no move?

Both I pray the days and nights
In their endless weary procession
Soon overwhelm my sad obsession

You and I
We've seen it all
Chasing our hearts' desire
But we go on pretending
Stories like ours
Have happy endings

Anatoly You could not give me
More than you gave me
Why should there be something in me
Still discontented?

Florence I won't look back anymore
And if I do — just for a moment

Anatoly I'll soon be happy to say I knew you then

Both But if you hear today
I'm no longer quite so devoted
To this affair, I've been misquoted

You and I
We've seen it all
Chasing our hearts' desire
But we go on pretending
Stories like ours
Have happy endings

They hold each other for the final time, then separate

Molokov, Svetlana and the Russian delegates arrive. Eventually Anatoly joins them and leaves with them to board a plane. Soon after they are gone, Walter arrives at the airport

Walter So in the end our hero won
Brilliantly!
Surprised us all —
He played as well as he has ever done

Florence No surprise.

Walter Well, this is:
He's just announced he's going back
To the Soviet Union.
He seems unable to win
Without the added thrill of changing sides

Pause. No response from Florence

Song 35: "Walter and Florence"

Don't you have a single word to say?

Florence No. No, you wouldn't listen anyhow
And what I'm feeling now
Has no easy explanation
Hasn't this been a great achievement?
Losing your man and nothing in return!

Walter Not my man — your man. Anyway, Anatoly's return to the Soviet bosom is a very decent gesture, if I may say so — he has virtually guaranteed us — er, you — your father. He must have done it for you, he wouldn't have done it for me.
Don't be so quick to put us down
We'll get your father out soon
That is, as long as he is still alive

Florence What? What did you say?

Walter (*backing away*) Well, we can't be *sure* that he's alive, but you couldn't be sure that he was dead, so you're no worse off ...

He sidles out

Florence Playing games — using our lives for nothing!

EPILOGUE

The Company enters

Song 36: "Epilogue"

Florence How to survive them?
Where do I start?
Let man's petty nations tear themselves apart
My land's only borders lie around my heart

CURTAIN

OPTIONAL MUSIC

"Someone Else's Story"

Florence

Long ago
In someone else's lifetime
Someone with my name
Who looked a lot like me
Came to know
A man and made a promise
He only had to say
And that's where she would be
Lately although her feelings run just as deep
The promise she made has grown
Impossible to keep
And yet I wish it wasn't so
Will he miss me if I go?

In a way
It's someone else's story
I don't see myself
As taking part at all
Yesterday
A girl that I was fond of
Finally could see the writing on the wall
Sadly she realized she'd left him behind
And sadder than that she knew
He wouldn't even mind
And though there's nothing left to say
Would he listen if I stay?

It's all very well to say
You fool, it's now or never
I could be choosing
No choices whatsoever

I could be
In someone else's story
In someone else's life
And he could be in mine
I don't see
A reason to be lonely
I could take my chances
Further down the line
And if that girl I knew should ask my advice
Oh I wouldn't hesitate
She needn't ask me twice
Go now!
I'd tell her that for free
Trouble is, the girl is me
The story is, the girl is me

"You and I/The Story of Chess"

Anatoly Knowing I want you
Knowing I love you
I can't explain why I remain
Careless about you
Florence I've been a fool to allow
Dreams to become great expectations
Anatoly How can I love you so much yet make no move?
Both I pray the days and nights
In their endless weary procession
Soon overwhelm my sad obsession

You and I
We've seen it all
Chasing our hearts' desire
But we go on pretending
Stories like ours
Have happy endings

Anatoly You could not give me
More than you gave me
Why should there be something in me
Still discontented?
Florence I won't look back anymore
And if I do — just for a moment
Anatoly — what you did then ——
Both But if you hear today
I'm no longer quite so devoted
To this affair, I've been misquoted

You and I
We've seen it all
Chasing our hearts' desire
But we go on pretending
Stories like ours
Have happy endings

Chorus

Each game of chess means there's one less
Variation left to be played
Each day got through means one or two
Less mistakes remain to be made

Not much is known
Of early days of chess beyond a fairly vague report
That fifteen hundred years ago two princes fought,
Though brothers, for a Hindu throne

Their mother cried
For no-one really likes their offspring fighting to the death
She begged them stop the slaughter with her every breath
But sure enough one brother died

Sad beyond belief
She told her winning son
You have caused such grief
I can't forgive this evil thing you've done

He tried to explain
How things had really been
But he tried in vain
No words of his could mollify the Queen

And so he asked the wisest men he knew
The way to lessen her distress
They told him he'd be pretty certain to impress
By using model soldiers on
A chequered board to show it was his brother's fault
They thus invented chess

Chess displayed no inertia
So spread to Persia, then west
Next the Arabs refined it,
Thus redesigned, it progressed

Still further yet
And when Constantinople fell in fourteen fifty-three
One would have noticed every other refugee
Included in his bags a set

Once in the hands
And in the minds of
Leading figures of the Renaissance
The spirit and the speed of chess
Made swift advance
Through all of Europe's vital lands

Where, we must record
The game was further changed right across the board
The western touch upon the
Pieces ranged

King and queen and rook
And bishop, knight and pawn
All took on the look
We know today, the modern game was born

And in the end
We see a game that started by mistake in Hindustan
And boosted in the main by what is now Iran
Become the simplest and most complicated
Pleasure yet devised
For just the kind of mind
Who would appreciate this well-researched
And fascinating yarn

Florence This is an all too familiar scene
Anatoly Hopeless reflections on what might have been
Both From all sides the incessant and burning question:
Florence "Bearing in mind your predicament now ——
Anatoly — what you did then ——
Both — we're just dying to know would you do it all again?"
Chorus Each day we get through means one less mistake there for the making

Both

But they know full well
It's not hard to tell
Though my heart is breaking
I'd give the world for that moment with you
When we thought we knew
That our love would last
But the moment passed
With no warning, far too fast

You and I
We've seen it all
Chasing our hearts' desire
But we go on pretending
Stories like ours
Have happy endings

FURNITURE AND PROPERTY LIST

ACT I

Scene 1

Off stage: Camera (**Frederick**)

Scene 2

On stage: Computer

Off stage: Newspapers (**Florence**)
Television cameras, paparazzi equipment (**Reporters**)

Scene 3

On stage: Television
Newspapers
Chess set

Scene 4

No props

Scene 5

On stage: Table
Two aluminium chairs
Chess set

Personal: **Florence:** handbag containing a piece of paper

Scene 6

No props

Scene 7

No props

SCENE 8

On stage: Microphone (practical)
Florence's coat

Personal: **Florence:** piece of paper

SCENE 9

No props

SCENE 10

Re-set as for Scene 5

SCENE 11

Personal: **Arbiter:** envelope

SCENE 12

On stage: Papers
Stamps
Ink pads

SCENE 13

On stage: Paparazzi equipment for **Reporters**

ACT II

SCENE 1

No props

SCENE 2

On stage: Television
Telephone

SCENE 3

On stage: Chess set
Gong
Glasses
Telephone
Envelope containing letter

SCENE 4

On stage: Sheet of paper
Sofa
Television cameras
Television
Video of **Svetlana**

Personal: **Anatoly:** clip-on microphone

SCENE 5

On stage: Telephone

Personal: **Florence:** document

SCENE 6

No props

SCENE 7

Personal: **Anatoly:** note
Frederick: pocket chess set

SCENE 8

On stage: Television
Chess set
Table
2 chairs

SCENE 9

No props

LIGHTING PLOT

Property fitting required: nil
Interior and exterior settings

To open: General overall lighting

ACT I, PROLOGUE
No cues

ACT I, SCENE 1 Train Station
No cues

ACT I, SCENE 2 Hotel suite/Conference room
No cues

ACT I, SCENE 3 Hotel suite
No cues

ACT I, SCENE 4 Arbiter's chambers
No cues

ACT I, SCENE 5 Chess arena
No cues

ACT I, SCENE 6 Chess arena
No cues

ACT I, SCENE 7 Chess arena
No cues

ACT I, SCENE 8 TV control room
No cues

ACT I, SCENE 9 Restaurant/Mountaintop
No cues

ACT I, Scene 10 Chess arena
No cues

ACT I, Scene 11 Hotel suite/Arbiter's chambers
No cues

ACT I, Scene 12 Embassy
No cues

ACT I, Scene 13 Train station
No cues

ACT II, Scene 1 Bangkok, Thailand
No cues

ACT II, Scene 2 Hotel suite
No cues

ACT II, Scene 3 Hotel suite
No cues

ACT II, Scene 4 TV studio
No cues

ACT II, Scene 5 Hotel foyer (chessboard)
No cues

ACT II, Scene 6 Hotel foyer (chessboard)
No cues

ACT II, Scene 7 Buddhist temple
No cues

ACT II, Scene 8 Chess arena
No cues

ACT II, Scene 9 Chess arena
No cues

EFFECTS PLOT

ACT I

Cue 1 Whistling/yodelling/orchestral interlude (Page 5)
Train rushes through the station

Cue 2 **Mayor and Citizens:** "... your life in a show ..." (Page 5)
Train rushes into the station and stops

Cue 3 To open Scene 2 (Page 7)
Computer voice says "Knight D-five"

ACT II

Cue 4 **Anatoly** changes channels (Page 42)
Abba singing "Money Money Money"

Cue 5 **Anatoly** switches back to **Frederick** (Page 42)
Cut music

Cue 6 **Anatoly** and **Florence:** "... My happy ending" (Page 44)
Telephone rings

Cue 7 To open Scene 3 (Page 44)
Anatoly's and Florence's last speeches are repeated

Cue 8 **Anatoly** enters (Page 56)
Sound of chanting monks

Cue 9 Beginning of Song 32 (Page 56)
Fade chanting

MADE AND PRINTED IN GREAT BRITAIN BY
LATIMER TREND & COMPANY LTD PLYMOUTH
MADE IN ENGLAND